AF571897

GANDHI'S LAP

GANDHI'S LAP

Charlotte Gould Warren

The Word Works
Washington, DC

First Edition.
First Printing.
Gandhi's Lap

The WORD WORKS,
PO Box 42164,
Washington, DC 20015.

Cover Art: "Himalayas," watercolor
by Charlotte Gould Warren

Book design, typography by Janice Olson

Printed in the USA.

Library of Congress Control Number 00-133731
International Standard Book Number: 0-915380-46-3

ACKNOWLEDGMENTS

Grateful acknowledgment is made to the following periodicals in which a number of poems first appeared in earlier versions.

The Literary Review: "India: Silver."

Mankato Poetry Review: "Gandhi's Lap."

Crosscurrents: "Finding a Language," "Digging."

The Spoon River Review: "There Were Barking Deer in the Hills."

Peninsula College Forum: "Shelter," "What Did I Expect?" "Savitri."

Writers' Harvest: "Making It Sing," "Olympic Peninsula Music Festival," "Light."

The Raven Chronicles: "You Can Count On It."

the eleventh Muse: "Over the Edge."

With thanks to Alice Derry for essential help with these poems, for her attentive heart and sustaining friendship; to the community of writers I am fortunate to work with; to Margaret McHugh, and a lifetime of caring teachers: in high school, Helen Young, in college, Kenneth Hanson, Nelson & Beth Bentley, and in graduate school, Mark Cox, David Rivard and, especially, Betsy Sholl whose work and spirit keep lighting the way. I am grateful to Word Works for the Washington Prize which has supported poets for over 20 years, to Karren Alenier for welcoming me, and to editor, Hilary Tham, whose quick mind and kind heart made our correspondence a pleasure.

"My Ariel, chick... Be free, and fare thou well."

—THE TEMPEST

"I mean, affectionate like violins
pitiless and brave
like children who can't talk yet,
ready to die as easily as birds
or live a thousand years."

—Nazim Hikmet
translated by Randy Blasing & Multlu Konuk

CONTENTS

I

I Meant To Tell You ~ 12

Gandhi's Lap ~ 14

In The Side Mirror ~ 16

Digging ~ 18

India: Silver ~ 20

Against My Disbelief ~ 21

Shelter ~ 23

Resistance ~ 25

Savitri ~ 27

Knife ~ 29

Breaking The Combs ~ 31

There Were Deer Barking In The Hills ~ 33

You Can Count On It ~ 37

The Party ~ 39

Looking Back ~ 40

II

Martha's Letter ~ 44

Moth-Eyes ~ 46

Everything Traveling In The Mind Resides ~ 47

Light ~ 49

Words ~ 50

Making It Sing ~ 51

Country Wife ~ 53

What Did I Expect ~ 55

Barely Visible ~ 57

Over The Edge ~ 58

India: Smoke ~ 59

Coming of Age ~ 60

Driving Home ~ 61

Finding A Language ~ 63

Cat's Eyes ~ 65

Flying ~ 68

After Elizabeth Bishop ~ 70

With My Back To The Window ~ 71

Leisure World ~ 72

•

About the Author ~ 75

for George
whose love makes all the difference

and for our sons
Carl & Todd

I MEANT TO TELL YOU

". . .I Have Been Stunned. Stand Back!"

—Walt Whitman

I meant to run downstairs and tell you,
drawing the curtains
against the cold,

that the dark
swagger of trees,
the pitch and furrow

of cedars, that clip
of moon, seemed—How can I say it?—
unexpected.

The way so small a bird, a dipper,
walks underwater
against the weight of current.

However often I've seen one,
it catches me off guard.
Bobbing there on a boulder,

it walks right into the crush
of water, taking the sky with it
in a silver cluster of bubbles.

I meant to say, Come, look!—
calling you up from the basement
where you rough-sanded an odd, bright button

fallen apart in my hands—
a button you glued
to its backing, the surface

an inlaid iridescence. The sky
was the way we first found it together,
pulling the dark

like a blanket up to our ears—stars
golden as crumbs
swept from the table. I meant to say

hurry! but the phone rang,
or I finished drawing our napkins
through the lacquered

rings I had searched for
in the dusty tin-sided shop
of childhood.

Why do I love what is so
far behind me, carried like a keepsake
to where I discover you

under the ordinary
hundred-watt bulb
in your cuff-worn shirt, a bit of luminescence

perched between your fingers?
And did I ever tell you? Or was it,
by then, too late?—the madrona

roughed matter-of-factly in a bolt of wind,
the way the dipper
walked against the current,

picking up periwinkles—
small pieces of the world
we promised each other.

GANDHI'S LAP

for Shunkar

Because his smile was as silly as his ears
I sat on Gandhi's lap and played with his pocket watch,
its weight glossed and ticking in my hand, certain
the Mahatma's voice and Dad's
would settle the world

the way the old soft-footed
nightwatchman swinging his lantern
unwound the dark like a turban
while I slept under a mosquito net.

Missionary-poor, fifth generation
Americans with servants, we felt at home.
I sang to my doll while Myku
swept his bundle of sticks

over the hard-packed ground.
Dust flew up with the scratchy leaves
from vines on the wide stone veranda, his body
bent like the branches of trees.

Long before we woke,
Shunkar nicked a wooden match with his thumbnail,
cupped the flame to kindling,
blew through the pipe of his fingers

to quicken the coals.
I learned that too,
watching, as under his knife
the grapefruit opened its jewelled eye,

the plucked chicken
flew headless from his hands,
feathers spattering the packed dirt courtyard.
Sullen afternoons he sat on the kitchen step

rolling a cigarette,
his gaze distant as smoke
unravelling in the jacaranda.
Even now it blinds me,

the white-washed glare of history,
how he never ate at our table,
how all those ayas, only girls themselves,
carried us flaxen-haired children on their hips.

We took them for granted, heedless
that their god Shiva
turned river water holy, and turtles
scavenged the dead.

All day men harnessed to barges
heaped with salt and millet
pulled against the sun.
Evenings, Shunkar,

grasping the rim with a dishtowel,
carried deep metal pans of boiling water
carefully through the house for our baths.
Steam jeweled his forehead, stained armpits.

The old house still stands, lived in
by others, while light pours like water,
keeps pouring over questions
I hadn't yet learned to ask.

IN THE SIDE MIRROR

"Out here, the weather"
—Greg Pape

Out here, the weather is golden as peaches
my mother lines up in glass jars
shelved in the one unheated
bedroom she saves for them.
On the next shelf, pickled beets.
Order holds down panic.

But even now, hiking the high
meadows through mountain grass turned bitter-sweet,
last week's bad dream stalks me: that man
in my car's side mirror
sauntering behind me, skinny, long-legged,
black coat flap-dancing,

keeps closing in.
His smile's sardonic, as if he owned the world,
face chalky and angular, eyes
not even bothering to track me.
I speed up to shake him,
gun the corner, skidding, but he just keeps

gaining ground—unhurried,
unyielding—until my rolled-up
window darkens, his body
blotting out mine.
The way a child shouts *Mother!* I wake,
gasping for someone. But why

would she hear me? Order
is what she was praised for,
couldn't get enough of, the need

to sterilize jars, line them up—
hard evidence against the sticky
skins, the pits crammed under

the garbage can's lid
someone else trucks away monthly.
As if that could protect her--
from the mother who died young,
the father who farmed out his children,
later, her own husband stealing into their daughter's bed.

What turns a woman powerless in her own home?
Some days I cut fresh roses the way she did,
clean counters and floors, herd dust
into delicate heaps the least draft scatters.
Other days, the man like the weather, the heat,
the low clouds, closes in.

DIGGING

I weight the steel by hopping,
feel through my arms the roots' resistance
to the tapered blade, hear
the tearing apart, the heft
of what I unearth: ripple of spiders
scuttle of beetle and grub.

I can see my mother now
hunched over the ground,
a dark cloud spitting at the weeds,
hissing at them with her shears.
If I could be that angry
I'd dig it all back up, the past

like a ruined garden, bare roots, blunt rocks,
Quack grass snapping as I lift a hunk of sod,
bang it on the ground, spring the pale
roots free, its ribbony blades
crowding tough and too gorgeous
to throw on the compost.

I hear the same confusion
in the song sparrow's cry over three spotted eggs
too close to the ground—one fledgling
killed by a cat, one egg carried off at night,
the other I retrieved, too late, rinsed and kept
in a dish of stones. It was that muddling connection

between grace and terror
I brought to the digging,
trying to make sense of a mother's talent
for finding fault and insisting on beauty.
We breathed her scolding the way these limp
live bodies of earthworms seem to breathe dirt.

I lean on the shovel,
the suddenness of beetles, bright-backed
as river rock, glinting iridescence
over the clods they climb, vulnerable
as a child stepping from the tub
carrying herself to where she thinks it's safe.

INDIA: Silver

One boat here, one
farther off, each
a dark cut-out

stunning the moonlit river.
Split bamboo poles
ten or twelve feet long,

hinged and strung
for the catch,
arch over the water.

The men
work their arms
like mimes

or puppeteers.
We drift—
timeless—

the whisper
of lifted nets,
the splash of drops

around us:
shudder
of caught fish,

bits and pieces
of moonlight—
small bodies thumping.

AGAINST MY DISBELIEF

Days before he moved—
hauling the noisy mower, the couches, fake deer,
the wife, plump and tanned, who liked
gardening in a bikini, swelling the house
with china umbrella holders, gilt-edged mirrors,
cauliflower-white carpeting she made him stay off of—
days before we could sigh good riddance,
my neighbor threw the Mountain beaver's body
on the compost. Gone,

how we used to stand, whispering, barefoot,
this side of the window. Gone, the hope
to see what emerged, unwinding its shaggy path
through the long wet grass to the Douglas fir. Gone,
the glimpse, the bristle of fur, wet nose held high, teeth clamped
on a branch dragged sideways, the whole
contraption in a tumble, disappearing to the yank and wag
of Nootka rose. O.K., so
it sabotaged our neighbor's hard-won

carrots, gnawed through tomato plants, and, years
before the house was built, riddled
Cline irrigation ditch, flooding
a little meadow: *Apolodontia.*
But, what am I to look at now
past what I know? Surely, we need more
than a disappearing
grass snake or a boulder washed down
from the ice age, to not feel fenced in.

This year the elk near town
came down to their ancient feeding grounds—
or maybe to protest K-Mart—stopping

the tourists on Highway 101, stopping
us, too, until, tranquilized,
they were lifted with nets,
trucked out to keep them
from trampling new gardens,
farmers' fences, seeded fields.

I don't want to be spitting mosquitoes
in the Amazon. Still, those
rackety birds, gaudy as Toucans,
that mile-high canopy of trees swayed
by monkeys, the drench
and slither of life in a bedlam
of green—maybe even the pug mark
of a leopard—wouldn't that abundance
be something worth waking to?

SHELTER

Allahabad
The civet cat's musk
is used as perfume

Shotguns broken open
over their arms, they stand
under the cottonwood,
heads tipped back, trying
to see through
the heart-shaped leaves,
each man shouting
as if he alone
has witnessed Vishnu
snared in the branch-clutter, refusing
to fall.

The child
drawn outside by the ruckus
glimpses fur,
something pulling itself
up, then jerked aside
as if by a hand.

When she sees it again,
hauling itself even higher
before slipping,
it seems to her

to fall
is the heart's
only way.

She, too,
might be hunted, treed,

her body's weight
on the curved nails,
the roof of her mouth
bony and fear-bitten.
Little by little,

her own life
could be
forced down.

When the last shot
finds its mark,
what thumps to the dust at their feet,
blood-matted, teeth bared,
seems so small a thing,
even the hunters
whose shouts had cracked open
the sky,
hardly know what to make
of the handful
in the dirt, and simply
walk away.

RESISTANCE

It was, finally, the image of the woman
in her old overcoat,
hit by mortar, dumped before
our eyes onto the plain
stone square, followed by
glasses of water in a circle
on the polished table
men had drawn their chairs to,
teeth, white cuffs, smiling
into the t.v. cameras.

If not that woman,
another. If not those men,
these—camouflaged, but differently
behind bazookas, blasting ancient
hand-built buildings, wasting
cabbages and marigolds,
picking off children.
Who will feed your old father,
woman running across
the city square for food, your two

boys and a girl, your half-mad
neighbor, now that you're a heap
of not-running? Mostar! The lovely
bridge is shattered. The curved labor
of hands. The lovely
bodies of buildings,
of mothers and men. To the camera
a child says, *Tell Them to Just*
Stop Fighting! I try
putting myself behind a gun

telescopic eye targeting
people like ants,
only I don't want to be there. I try
lacing up their boots on my feet, stomp
on a stomach, set fire . . .For what?
I think of Akhmatova.
Even her poems,
hurled like grenades,
don't save us, didn't save
her country, that woman.

SAVITRI

for the cook's wife
in the Himalayas

That's where I found you,
scrubbing a cook pot
with a clump of grass I might have
used when I pulled myself up
taking shortcuts from school.

Light from the kitchen
barely reached us.
In the prowling dark, your wrists
in their busy bracelets
turned everything easy. None of it was.

Not the grit and guzzle
of sandy water, not the raw smell
of dirt wrapped up in roots.
I still feel hillsides
inside a bowl grating with stones.

Drenched and sparkling
in the widening spiral of throw-away light,
gravel scatters me back to childhood's
cottage in the mountains, its small square windows
crowded with stars. Soon enough

someone would call me to bed.
Whatever was warmth,
whatever spilled
from the back of the house,
you knew to stand

on difficult stones,
tucking your sari
from the splatter and murk.
I thought you were old. You were sixteen—
just sixteen.

KNIFE

1950's

A doctor himself,
my uncle wouldn't
touch her—although he was
kind. He warned
not to use names, to take cash—
three hundred dollars—
earned bussing dishes for college,
the tips counted out
at the wobbly table
of our upstairs rental.

It felt good saving her
instead of feeling lost myself.
At nineteen, she went on
loving the boyfriend
who punched her in the stomach,
and then had her
drink cheap whiskey and ipecac.
I phoned the only relative
I hoped I could count on, drove her to Seattle,
the number my uncle gave me

hidden deep in a pocket.
Afterward, where else could I take her
but to my folks' house? I wanted them
to comfort her. Instead, mother's voice
lashed out. Face drained,
eyes darkened, my friend never
let on she heard the shaming words,
dug in her purse
for something to protect her,
fumbled past felt pens, car keys,

to the red and white flip-top box
she offered me. We both lit up.
Missionaries, my parents,
like most people, feared
what the neighbors
might think. We stayed the night,
then left. But I was as dumb
as they were, never asking
what if my friend had bled to death
in the car, what if the car

had broken down?
It's that knife I tried
to come to terms with
all these years loving children
into their own lives.
A knife
that jimmies open
each cell of the body, alert now
to breaking and entering the once-
wide windows where someone

used to breathe easy. The knife
of being a woman, inhabiting a body
others also call home,
not able simply
to walk away.

BREAKING THE COMBS

"Hold still, Sweetheart,"
he says to his child
when the honey bee
lands on her arm. She feels
its breathy wings on her wrist,
its curious feet.

It doesn't sting.

He picks leeches off her legs,
turns them unharmed
back to the pond
she swam in for fun, innocent
of sucking mouths,

moves the snake aside with a stick,
carries her home
when she falls asleep.

•

How can she know
the hands she loves
will some day steal
her body's lightness, rob,

for pleasure,
secrets
she never knew she had?

Breaking the combs
he smokes for honey,
sometimes he is stung.

Soda with a drop
of water in the palm,
soothes the venom.

"Hold still," he says.
She's there, but gone.

THERE WERE DEER BARKING IN THE HILLS

When was it—
in between the bridge's planks—

the river winked at me from below?
Not that blue

I'd seen from the porch,
but a sharpening of knives,

the way, stealth-footed,
dawn opens the doors.

•

Whistling, stropping your razor,
you were the father.

Mother slept late.
Star-flowered jasmine

spilled over the tile roof,
bougainvellia, trumpet vine.

Soon the light
would come.

•

Kishan served us
early breakfast—toast and tea

and half a grapefruit picked
from a tree in our garden.

Oh, it was sweet!

Just the two of us

on the porch at the wicker table
set with knives and sugar.

•

Still in bathrobes, sandals flapping,
we walked across the Jumna, the bridge

not yet crowded, the river far below us,
Allahabad, City of God,

creaking awake on its wooden wheels:
bullock carts, hoof clops, dark leather blinders,

the slow bells of oxen.
I skip-hopped beside you.

Soon the sun would rise,
crinkling the river to a maze of gold,

hiding deeper currents
where snapping turtles scavenged the dead.

•

Mother planted blousey sweet peas, marigolds,
larkspur bruised and iridescent,

colors she cut and carried indoors.
I wanted her to hold me.

•

Mahatma, intransitive verbs,
Mark Twain—

the students adored you.
Their saris and homespun

tied at the waist, you pitched them
basketballs, ran with the javelin,

its shaft shuddering
upright in earth.

I climbed the leathery limbs of the banyan
or watched from the game field, munching *chunna*.

•

Afternoons, I found you
at home at your desk, scribbling notes

on student papers, coaxing
sermons onto the page.

You lit a hand-rolled cigarette, pet crow
on your shoulder, mongoose

asleep in your tucked-in shirt.
Under the ceiling fan's

paddle of flies and sun motes,
I climbed into your lap.

•

When was it, you found me, still asleep,
slipped into my pajamas, insistent,

the way the deer's short barks,
hunted, came breathless?

Always, the day began again,
as if nothing had happened—

insects probing
the ghostly netting,

the hard wooden bed frame
I climbed over to the floor.

The way the sun bore down.

YOU CAN COUNT ON IT

"They will break your legs and insist you walk."
Marie Howe, The Good Thief.

In that world we turn away from,
where the sky opens like a sari
stretched between men's hands
over bare ground, heat
tightening

the threads of dyed cotton—
In that land where a man
can pull a woman
to him by unravelling
her sari,

where the river runs
forever, no matter the burning,
no matter the ashes and marigolds,
no matter the wailing hands it runs through
as if from thirst—

In that country-of-so-many,
where families lie on the grit of sidewalks,
a thin cloth their only roof and window,
their locked door and chimney—
In that courtyard,

they break your legs
on purpose,
so you can grow up begging,
so you can walk on your knees in the dirt,
holding your palms for coins.

Hunger
is what you count on—
its industry of children,
its bones
in the dust

or scattered by the river,
a childhood
under skies
savage
with beauty.

THE PARTY

She lay in a haze of mosquito netting
tucked under the blue and white
ticking, her child-bones weightless.

Mosquitoes whined on their whiskery legs
trying to get in. She watched them, half-awake.
When the door spilled its wedge of light,

when the murmur of guests, their laughter, surged
pebble-like as surf, *Mother*, she said,
remembering her mother's Georgette dress, its dreamy

blackness beaded with pearls,
Evening In Paris brushing her cheek
with their goodnight kiss.

In the party's ascension, her mother soared,
bird-radiant, trailing and preening iridescence,
a momentary contentment she, too, shared.

That, and the undertow
of disappointment stinging like salt—the shining
floor, pressed linen, lilies speckle-throated, just-

opening, the green glass dishes
brought from high shelves, all, not
to be touched—even love

pulled out in a clatter and polished
like silverware,
glittering under houselights.

LOOKING BACK

I still feel your steady pull
on the oars, and how as you stroked,
you faced us,

your student's sari
breezy in the light, her barely-
perceptible fragrance.

It's an old story.
You were her professor.
Probably nothing much happened.

I must have been seven or eight, there
to cover for the outing.
How shyly I took in her beauty.

I can still feel our toes
touching yours, braced
on the wooden ribbing,

the slap and drag of paddles,
the knocking of shafts
in their oarlocks, a commotion

of light in her bracelets.
When the shipped oars drained
and we drifted, it wasn't your voice

reading Browning that held me
but the river's rhyming and chiming,
the slosh of its resistance, riding

the cusps of waves to have a glance
over the edges,
you, forever looking back,

the two of us
looking forward.
I could have wished

for the surface dazzle
not to hide a deeper cold. But instead,
I felt chosen and happy to be along.

It took lifetimes,
pulling against the sheen,
to realize I was just a convenience.

That however we counted on you for love,
in the end, you took
what you wanted, always the tender

betrayer. And the river
so blue, was, even then,
polluted. We drifted near the white sand banks

as they slipped in and out
of the current, dissolving and re-forming
their shapely revision of rivers.

When the noon-daggered surface
turned brash, we moved inside
for shelter.

II

MARTHA'S LETTER

for Martha, Sigrid, Gertie & Oscar,
& for Sophia Olson & Frances Peterson

I remember more about Mama than Pa. I guess
she was home more, scrubbed sheets
on a washboard, heated the iron on a stove,
steamed and mashed pumpkin from the garden
for pies. She bore him five children, the last one
still-born, took in washing, cried a lot for Sweden.
Pa loved the garden, labeled each row,
yelled sometimes, hit us, broke a platter once.
When Mama worked at Farnstalk's,
she took me with her. I liked hearing the train whistle.
The man who lifted the crossing gate
told stories, gave me an apple.
Pa worked the coal yards in Katonah. Drove
a team of horses. He took the chute
with him, the coal clatter-banging
into other people's basements, came home
to chop wood, weed the onions. We raised
chickens, gathered nuts to dry in the attic.
Over time, their green covers blackened,
ready for us to peel. Mama never learned English, had us kids
translate, wrote her letters home in Swedish.
Mama had a fur hat, wore it to church Christmas. She and Pa
took me. Even without the words, she loved the songs,
the service. The tree shone like Mama's eyes
the once-in-a-while she laughed. Our tree had real candles.
I could string the popcorn. After the baby died,
Mama wandered the streets, crying, tore at her clothes,
once took them off. Pa sent me to fetch her and I was
ashamed, bringing her back. Once in a borrowed sled, for fun,
she and Pa pushed me. Another time—
when was it?—we all sat down to dinner,

Mama wasn't there, I went looking,
found her in the bathroom,
feet inside the tub, shoes and stockings dangling,
both legs cut, both wrists, deep with Pa's razor.
"Does it hurt, Mama?"
"No," she said.
Then Pa came in. Chased me away; later
sent Gertie to tell me Mama'd been taken—
three men in a black car. I remember a game we played—
"Hit The Cat"—two sticks, the short one
balanced on an edge. We whacked it
with the long one, laid the long stick
end over end to measure how far
the short one was kicked.

MOTH-EYES

She was
that kind of child—
easily dazzled, playful,
banging again and again
against the crib rails
of containment
dutiful daughters
are groomed for.
Her furry wings,
trapped in others' hands,
quieted at last
to stare with marked
incurable eyes
at a world already
shut down.

EVERYTHING TRAVELING OUT OF THE MIND RESIDES

Himalayas, 1940's

The world tuned in when Hillary and Tenzing
planted flags, and the Chinese
pushed their borders closer, but for me
it was home and wholly mine.
Each rock was alive, our bruises not of their making.
We ran, my brother and I, from sharper tongues
through deodar and mountain grass
to *Oly Oly Oxen Free* and *Kick The Can.*

Nothing was named: blade, wing and stem
stayed perfectly themselves. Mornings,
moss steamed in the oaks
wet as the wings of Rhinocerous beetles, evenings spilled
alizarin crimson over the sheen of distant rivers.
We let the world invent us,
the way at ten thousand feet, calling
through cupped hands, one man to another,

coolies relayed messages valley to valley,
all the steep way home.
Harnessed to tump lines and ninety-pound loads,
they greeted us children with soft-spoken words,
leg muscles taut. Once I saw a piano
moving through the woods
strapped to someone's back, the cook's
comment, *By thirty he'll be dead.*

Each year at Zig Zag—that mountain cottage
loaned by the mission—the honey-man found us.
I never thought of him as poor, or felt
the weight of gallon cans

biting his back up steep, dry hills. He unwound his turban
to strain the honey through it—
sweet thick ropes of shimmering gold—
leaf-bits and twigs caught in the folds.

I watched him hold the hand-scales up,
metal links tensing
to bear the jar of light—tapping out
monsoon's clatter in the Fall
on the tin roof of our room, my brother and I
asleep, soothed by the drumming dark.
Holidays, we trekked or were carried
to Deosari. I sat high up

in the sway of a creaking *kundi,* black-faced
Lungoors peering down from the oaks.
They surged the tree-tops
a hundred at a time, wave
after wave, quiet as dream,
little ones wrapped in the keep
of an arm. We dammed
streams to plunge pools, shook

dust from our socks, slept while the coolies
banked their fire against the bitter night, the big
cats' prowl; never thought to wonder
what was at risk, or what invisible weights we carried.
Those frost-hardened mornings
sun warmed apricots strewn on the ground—
furry fruit, small enough for a child to hold,
the juice on our chins sticky and sweet.

Kundi: shoulder basket
Lungoors: Himalayan monkeys

LIGHT

Allahabad

There was a time when her father—her head
heavy against his shoulder—
carried her into the front yard's
dusk to see the stars. They opened

hazy-winged as moths
shivering against the screen door of the sky
before he swung her back to bed, her own hands
already loosened by sleep.

Light closes its eyes the way a child does
falling into the velvet pouch of night,
muffling and distancing
the clank of insects, jackals' yap and moan,
shifting cattle.

To the whipoowill's call,
the returning
mumble of owls.

What happened next
always came as a surprise—
light opening her eyes—cat's gloss
stepping through snapdragons,

water unwinding itself from the tap. Light
held out its shimmering bowl,
pooled under the porch, dappled

and swinging overhead in the leaves
while she balanced the spoon,
bringing it to her lips.

WORDS

When he came
and the sticky smell
stuck to her child-skin
she was pinned like a moth
to the pitch of his words
telling her he loved her
and she was his joy,
his voice thick
and resonant in the half-dawn
of what would become
her life.

Not that she didn't grow up,
grow away, fall into—
maybe even head over heels
into—love, into sex as it should be
and rapture,

but *She Who Watches*
still cries out, and *She Who Turns Away*
still keeps leaving, breaking
what falls through her fingers like water,
like ash. *She Who Lights*
The Match still goes up in flames.
A commotion of wings
where her body sticks to the ground.
And then, like a belt,
the words rain down.

Guardian of Native Americans in her village,
She Who Watches *still looks over us from a*
petroglyph on the banks of the Columbia river.

MAKING IT SING

I'm so damn monogamous.
Just when I'm ready to run away
I love you all over again.
When I was young and men's eyes

followed me, I knew a housewife,
a woman forever waxing linoleum
in a run-down brownstone
off forty-second street,

the shine covered with newspaper
to catch footprints, her voice
brash and practical
dishing up the pasta her son

handed to me, the girl he'd brought home,
strutty as a mountain bird
puffed up to mate.
I hardly knew how she loved me,

but even her lumbago,
the soot and heat, the price of lox
were given into my keeping.
She went right on scolding

or laughing at the joke
she'd heard in the garment district
where she found me a dress just the right color.
Looking into her eyes

I thought of her married over thirty years,
still on her hands and knees. But here I am

on a floor across country,
making the same moves

glossed with summer sunshine,
with bird call, and not the grit of traffic
or break-dancing sidewalks,
exotic as she found my past—

a child waking up in India
to temple bells swaying
like the trunks of elephants.
Not her life on forty-second street,

but the herd of elephants
circling to shelter their newborn. What must it
have felt like, looking through that forest of legs
to the shimmering world beyond?

You're a lovely *goy*,
she told me, but should marry
one of your kind. And I did—for different
reasons—missing,

not her son,
but her own rowdy, undisguised
affection, her nudge and sway
of survival,

a woman I wanted once
never to be like—loud-mouthed, frowzy—
the very kind my voice calls back now,
to make of the daily something fabulous.

COUNTRY WIFE

Those days you let me off
at 5th and Pine before scouting
used car lots, I pretended
I wasn't really shopping.
Shopping was for women
unloved and rich—
but I loved all of it—the glass
counters full of silk
scarves and cosmetics, wildly
colorful leather
handbags, the bored
salesgirls with scarlet
lips, and matrons
with tired serious eyes. I loved
the elevator man, white-gloved
on automatic, the doorman
with brassy tassles
on slap-stick epaulets,
my own padded shoulders
and best dress, my gloves
smelling of kidskin. It's gone now.
The store, the gloves,
the desire—mostly. But back then
I'd ride the marble wall
reflecting all of us together, a moving
freize of hope and strangers.
Stepping off onto the carpet's big 5
I'd browse Steubens and Dansk, wonder
what kind of fiery glass-blower
blew Jonah into the luminous whale,
who cut down teak in what shadowy forest
for ice buckets and salad bowls
I lifted and stroked. I couldn't say then
if what tugged at me was longing,

if I felt endangered by shopping
or rescued. Shoes tipsy-heeled,
wide hats, scarves like kisses,
I tried on satin nightgowns
your hands would marry.
Ooo, I was laced with price tags,
pleats, sass and silk.
Sad to put everything back
but the towels we needed
and a sale blouse held on my lap
on the curved stone
bench by the parking garage where I waited.
Lives kept coming towards me—
in high heels and polka dots,
Brooks Brothers' pinstripes, bluejeans—
brushing past the blind man's
dog and guitar on the sidewalk
to a clank of coins the passing strangers
dropped him. I can't quite name it.
Like history, there'd always be people
ready to replace me. Why had I imagined us
glossed and eternal—as if life was like that—
not daily and perfectable, not hungry—
daring me to walk off with that stranger
whose easy stride and uncluttered gaze
swept him to me, right into the abrupt
shock of recognition that actually it was you.
A head above the others,
more stunning than the doorman,
miraculously yourself, the way you still appear
in unexpected light.
Driving home, I turn the dial
past opera's formal arias,
looking for something more intimate,
in my lap the black panties
and bra I bought
against need and judgement.

WHAT DID I EXPECT?

for our son Carl

Why would your wife want to protect you?
Why would you let her? Your hands,
as you speak, move in the air like kestrels
testing a leather wrist, or like fingers laced

in a spiral of phone cord, waiting for words.
Here at the restaurant, you draw your father out—
finances, weather, torque—
things he's at ease with, hoping instead

for his feelings, a current you could enter.
What did I expect? How you'd bring me
grass whistles, berries from thicketed fields,
plunked in my lap as if it were home. Not this abstract

affection, neat as a column of figures, however steady.
Outside, the new moon
balances on a larkspur. Such essential ease!
You're under your wife's spell now,

golden tints in her hair,
curls touching her earrings, brightening
her shoulders, just out of our reach,
a quick mind. Maybe I talk too much.

Forgive me.
I look out on the same fields you stood in as a boy,
tugging the sky by a string, feeling it
pull against you, the sun too curious

not to come close,
catching at the feet

of the soft-leaved alfalfa. I thought the world's
stubble and shine would protect you,

but even then you knew better, wanting us with you,
someone you could bump into, glance off of,
however we got in your way.
In this restaurant, light glances through ice cubes

to rainbow the wall.
No one's quite at ease—not us, your parents,
not you, our son. Your wife's shy voice
hands you in barely a whisper, words, maybe agreed on,

to keep you what?—neutral?—resistant to childhood's
backward pull?—as we would, first married,
calm ourselves with talk to stay less defensive with in-laws.
I suppose that's why it hurts. What did I expect?

That we would turn out better?
She unwraps a dinner mint as she listens,
creases the foil with her fingernails,
tears it to sixteen bits, as if to order our thinking,

as if to keep these countries with common borders
separate. What are any of us afraid of
but not measuring up, or failing each other with love
in the wrong proportion? The wind quits

or it's gusting. We want more
than letting go, than being reeled in,
something bigger than sky, the sheer give and dazzle
of risking each other.

BARELY VISIBLE

The sky threw back its silk-threaded
scarlet-and-gold blanket,
staining us with darkness.
Indoors, where the toaster glowed,
the amaryllis lily opened its purse
to a freckle of coins, fragrance trying
all the slot machines of the heart.
I set this down, period, but it walked away
with a mind of its own, including a little
dance of indecision on the brink
of discovery. What do you think?
Should I squash it, its one amazing life,
or let it climb into our futures,
stopping us mid-phrase, planting
its flag of an unknown country in whatever we think
we might have to say?

OVER THE EDGE

Himalayas

I must have been a keeper, Love,
because here we are still grounded,
living with a pine tree,
its long needles filtering all the stars
of the northern hemisphere sailing by
quietly night after night.
The earth, too, is ancient, its days overlapping,
tied at one end like the pine needles
my brother and I poked into hand-made bundles to sled on,
rushing the mountain trails.
Did I tell you of the boy who picked up so much speed
he just kept going, airborne,
falling and falling;
then, like a boulder, bounced,
not splitting apart
but whole, landing far below us, face-up,
pale and smooth as the tulip bulbs
I plant each spring, unbroken glasses,
shattered watch still ticking, stopped heart?
Maybe he was as homesick
and passionate as those of us left
to stare transfixed and shaking.
Here I am planting this pine tree
to remind me of him,
or not him, exactly, but what's unlived in each of us,
what could stand tall
and branch out roughly.
Grace seems to come from not knowing—
the way bark is innocent
of the clawed toes, the sharp beaks of creepers,
the sleek shoulders of nuthatches,
the flocking, piping siskins. Maybe that's why
I work here, on a deck I always wanted
to build, with a family I could count on
because I never quite had one.

INDIA: Smoke

Held between two sticks, the live coal
passes from hand
to hand. Men of the village

smoke in the quiet of evening,
each face, for a moment, lit by the glow,
Dhothies ghost-like

in the dusk. They sit together,
a circle of equals, something comfortable
as the second self.

At times, there is only
one cigarette. It makes
the rounds untouched

by lips, cupped between
hands, deeply inhaled.
What does it mean

that I've kept them with me—
these guardians
of the past, sweet

and acrid as smoke,
when all I've ever known of them
was a circle of distance?

dhothie: loose-fitting white cotton garment

COMING OF AGE

Finally, she is old enough
to run her arms into the deep
folds of silk saris
heavy on the shelf, satin half-slips—
weight of rivers,
of marigolds, hibiscus—the flowering
shapes of women.

DRIVING HOME

I love driving this small
solid car, speeding up
at the corners I used to slow down for,
moving from the outer
to the inner edge of the lane in one
smooth line through that S-curve
opening into the Dungeness valley—

foothills to the south,
Juan de Fuca to the north.
Every road goes somewhere.
But these stubble fields
resist us in their mystery. Dark shapes
nudging the landscape like spirits
must be cows—Holsteins

I could run my hands over;
one way rough as barns, the other
more like water over stone. Either way,
they'd stand there, maybe
shifting a bit. Back of the barns
are houses where mothers pour milk
into children's glasses,

and behind them, cupboards
hinting of crystal.
It's times like this, at dusk,
far things merge. Roadside litter
flips up to spook me,
pale as clam shells I drifted over in a canoe.
Back then, I knew I could step out and walk if I had to,

even if the cold numbed my feet, and the whole
salt bay pushed against me like a child.
But last summer when I jumped off that
boulder in Vermont, caught mid-life
between traction and longing,
I just wanted to plunge—
freefall, into the clear deep pool—

young again, intact,
like facing a fish-ladder in Seattle,
the other side of glass—
turbulence suddenly
clearing up vision, jetting a Silver,
then a Chinook into view, eye
to my eye in the current.

Crisp air flowing from the mountains
tugs the smoke of wood stoves
and slash fires out to sea.
I almost seem to know—
for the moment—I'm happy,
turning on the headlights,
bringing the rough ground near.

FINDING A LANGUAGE

for our son Todd

You could juggle anything—
oranges, tennis balls, one
conversation over another,
this job, that, the car,
the road, the car phone,
the cops, but not your assigned
order of birth, younger brother,
the two of you circling at Christmas,
mouths full of phrases
seeming to lead nowhere
until your hands
without thinking
picked up bean bags
easier than words, and
not to be outdone,
as if what was playful
had grown into challenge,
your brother joined in the intricate language—
three red, three blue—
expressions
too rapt to look into
while you shuffled
in your beat-up
gym shoes to the easy, unconscious,
unattended dancing
feet do
when hands knit the air invisibly
with cat's cradles or nothing in particular,
as if letting go and catching
were all the same
and all that mattered,
while, facing each other,

drawing closer,
without missing a beat or letting on,
you tossed one to him
and he caught and returned it neatly,
keeping
his own hands going,
a mystery none of us
wants to escape,
except by entering into.

CAT'S EYES

for my brother Bill

Pushing it in its track, I open the window
thinking about us as school kids in India, you boys
bunched around marbles, heads almost touching
as you palm the dirt smooth. The jolt

scatters the deer,
but when they see it's just me
they go back to licking each other behind the ears
and I return easily to the past.

You lean on an elbow to line up
each steely, intent as Grandfather taking aim
at a tiger. It was Grandfather
villagers sent their runners for

when a big cat dragged off
one of their children—Grandfather
keeping his own company,
fond of cigars, holding chairs for the ladies.

He'd sit in a blind,
not stirring for hours,
waiting for first light, for the grass blade's
shudder, a young goat

tied to the tree trunk, bleating.
Southern gentleman, preacher, his wife
a doctor, Grandfather
wasn't remembered

for sermons carefully crafted,
but for what he loved most—being a crack shot,

and afterwards, the stories.
You must have wanted that, too,

those few hard-won moments of approval,
compressed and lustrous,
weighted with promise. Even the air was pure then,
heavy with diesel decades later when I returned.

It took a long life
for me to get back. Himalayan hillsides
hadn't changed much. Pines
kept shaking out needles in the sun,

the old oaks looked stubborn.
What was left of the forest was guarded.
How passionately we had loved it!
As children, we really didn't have each other

and the servants kept changing.
Even now, we want back
what's lost—monsoon rains
thundering in the fall, calling up moss

thick as a bear's coat on the oaks,
not judging, just abundant.
I returned for one last look—hillsides
opening to black umbrellas, a girl

with matted hair whistling in the goats.
Ayas still dragged the childrens' bedding onto dorm
roofs to dry, still bent over metal tubs
to scrub small heads with lysol.

I've grown to like that smell, resinous
here in the pines, where today

on the living room rug my friend's little girl
dumps out all the marbles.

She doesn't want
to knock them into each other, or win.
She wants, over and over, to sort them—
the lupine blues here, the golden cat's eyes there,

paired and clustered into matched pools,
as if she could make sense of her mother and father—
slamming their pain on the table,
or speechless.

She places them side by side, at ease,
the way the deer bed down, her eyes
darkening and inward,
to make that happen.

FLYING

I step up jauntily into the cockpit
as if I were Lindberg, his son not yet kidnapped,
as if I were Amelia not yet vanished, the sky still shouting hello
no matter the weather. All our lives
we give ourselves up to strangers, squalling at birth
into the hands of an indifferent world,
this time into the co-pilot's seat of a Cessna
rising out of the cow pasture we shout over.
Rackety and shuddering
we lift through tidepools of night. Towns fall away
like bits of shimmering crustaceans
stashed at the foot of the mountains. The pilot's
short-sleeved white shirt glows, his arm
animal-steady, so close I can touch it.
He tells me his father bought him
lessons at nineteen, afraid
his life was going to hell in a hay basket—
meaning girls, fast cars, vodka. Hard to say
whether he slowed down or speeded up.
When he was nineteen, I was having
babies. What if I'd asked myself instead—Hey,
do I want to fly?
Assumed I was able, free.
Just thinking about it now,
how I raised kids, tower to bridge, my calm
air controller's voice to their head-on collisions,
or my hands like Mariott's packing food for United—
all those school lunches—
makes me realize he couldn't imagine
being there any more than I could imagine
talking into the head set—*gear up,*
flaps down—or my holding the wheel steady,
for our family

flying bumpily through stars in a steep terrain
northwest of Seattle where the great hooves of darkness
easily out-pace us, and against which
training and confidence don't stand a chance.

AFTER ELIZABETH BISHOP

Braving the blown grit of freeways,
braving the bottle shards and pop cans,
the cigarette butts, plastic bags and condoms,
the steep forest duff of the Olympic peninsula,
a cougar stalks a child in his own back yard,
a bear lounges in a California hot tub
coming down from the hills day after day
as if from a commute, a moose in Montana chews its cud
on a family's lawn. Like a child in hand-me-downs,
the moose wears a coat too big for itself,
and the school bus stops.
The door sighs open
on its pneumatic tracks, the driver
waits patiently, or impatiently.
Does the moose gather its four legs and huge
head, its bony bulk and shadow
into a battered seat? Maybe I'm not
suited, it thinks—big-boned swamp-wader—
to be crammed into rows,
and it glides along in its running gait
the way children once balanced books on their heads
to walk smoothly, flow from here to there, halting to browse,
crossing graveled rivers. Maybe, all along,
the moose doesn't want the bus,
wants an empty house instead,
stands there nibbling water lilies
pulled off the wall paper,
making us feel the wilderness
inside us, its strange grace,
its eyes that gaze like quiet rooms
pulling down a mouthful of whatever it likes to eat.

WITH MY BACK TO THE WINDOW

Gradually sun warms my shoulders,
casts a window of light
on the kitchen floor
where a woman like myself,
only darker, stretches—
arms, legs, torso.
There must be a lesson here.

But I turn,
balancing this blue and white
bowl of fresh oranges,
to face the sun itself.

Already
it singles out each tree, slips over
a maple, counts every thorn
on a thicket the winter wren sings through.
Soon it will reach the mosque-of-many-tulips,
leaves wide as prayer rugs tasseled with dew.
One by one by one.

LEISURE WORLD, LAGUNA HILLS

Planes tear the sky apart like sheets my friend and I
tore back then for bandages in girl scouts, earning
badges in earnest. But today we're here
under the tree that shades her husband's
ashes, its leaves shimmering,

mocking the Parkinson's
that killed him. She's busying herself
saving wetlands, frogs, Great Blues,
splashing down in watercolors
taught at the Leisure Center.

From her second floor balcony
I look into the crowns of trees
lost and found in sunlight. Again, today,
these sliding glass doors are closed
against the jackhammer's shudder, the leaf-blower's

shriek, our own voices pitched high, calling
"I can't hear you!" She pays
for the privilege of ordered lawns, for guards
at the gatehouse who wave
as if they knew us, not our windshield,

just as we pay to air-condition our bodies
down the smooth arcs of freeways where whole groves
of orange trees lie cut and stacked for cordwood,
or pay for corn and berries sprayed by white-suited
masked men walking the rows of our hunger.

In the distance, the skyline glints with its toy-block
buildings. Closer, two bare-legged boys in the scummy stream
hunt frogs. Again tonight, those frogs begin—

nasal and resinous. Their racket's full of bass notes
and sweet high pipings—a quagmire of collaboration

synchronized like the automatic sidewalk lamps
coming on to gather their galaxies
of gnats. Overhead,
on the soft bank of evening, a loudspeaker
plays dance music someone laughs through.

And why shouldn't they?
Why shouldn't my friend dip quickly
into cobalt, veridian, to catch the tremor of trees,
the way, tomorrow, I'll swim laps
as if kicking could save me?

ABOUT THE AUTHOR

Charlotte Warren's poems have appeared in journals such as *Seattle Review, Calyx, The Literary Review, Southern Poetry Review,* and *Kansas Quarterly,* as well as on Seattle's buses. Her book manuscript received recongnition in several national competitions: Cleveland State's, Southern Illinois University's *Crab Orchard Review,* Western Michigan's *New Issues Press,* and the University of Wisconsin's *Brittingham* series. *Gandhi's Lap* is her first published collection of poetry. Warren received her MFA from Vermont College, and teaches part time at Peninsula College in Port Angeles, Washington. Born of missionary parents, she grew up in India, and has made her home on Washington's Olympic peninsula. She is married and has two sons.

Gandhi's Lap is the winner of the 2000 Word Works Washington Prize. Charlotte Gould Warren's manuscript was selected from 385 manuscripts submitted by American poets.

FIRST READERS:
Barbara Alfaro
Nancy Allinson
Dean Blehert
Donald Cunningham
Bernadette Geyer
Patricia Gray
Andrea Gull
Erich S. Hintze
Cynthia Hoffman
James Hopkins
Tod Ibrahim
Brandon Johnson
Sydney March
Amy Jo Ross
Rhonda Williford
Marcella Wolfe

SECOND READERS:
Sally Murray James
Steven B. Rogers
Jonathan Vaile, Assistant Director

FINAL JUDGES:
Karren L. Alenier
J.H. Beall
Miles David Moore
Martha Sanchez-Lowery, Director
Hilary Tham

ABOUT THE WORD WORKS

The Word Works, a nonprofit literary organization, publishes contemporary poetry in collectors' editions. Since 1981, the organization has sponsored the Washington Prize, an award of $1,500 to a living American poet. Each summer, The Word Works presents free poetry programs at the Joaquin Miller Cabin in Washington, DC's Rock Creek Park. Annually, two high school students debut at the Miller Cabin Series as winners of the Young Poets Competition.

Since The Word Works was founded in 1974, programs have included: "In the Shadow of the Capitol," a symposium and archival project on the African-American intellectual community in segregated Washington, DC; the Gunston Arts Center Poetry Series (including Ai, Carolyn Forché, Stanley Kunitz, Linda Pastan, among others); the Poet-Editor panel discussions at the Bethesda Writer's Center (including John Hollander, Maurice English, Anthony Hecht, Josephine Jacobsen, among others); Poet's Jam, a multi-arts program series featuring poetry in performance; a poetry workshop at the Center for Creative Non-Violence (CCNV) shelter; the Writers' Retreat workshops and readings in Tuscany; and Café Muse at Strathmore Hall Arts Center. In 1997 The Word Works collaborated with Mica Press (Ft. Collins, Colorado) to distribute Mica's Premiere Series of literary chapbooks.

Past grants have been awarded by the National Endowment for the Arts, the National Endowment for the Humanities, the DC Commission on the Arts and Humanities, the Witter Bynner Foundation, and others, including many generous private patrons.

The Word Works has contributed artistic and administrative materials to the Washington Writing Archive housed in The George Washington University Gelman Library.

Please enclose a self-addressed stamped envelope with all inquiries. Find out more about The Word Works at:

http://www.wordworksdc.com

email: editor@wordworksdc.com

WORD WORKS BOOKS

Karren L. Alenier, *Wandering on the Outside*
Karren L. Alenier, ed., *Whose Woods These Are*
Karren L. Alenier, Hilary Tham, Miles David Moore, eds., *Winners: A Retrospective of the Washington Prize*
* Nathalie F. Anderson, *Following Fred Astaire*
J. H. Beall, *Hickey, The Days...*
Mel Belin, *Flesh That Was Chrysalis* (Capital Collection)
* Peter Blair, *Last Heat*
* John Bradley, *Love-In-Idleness*
Christopher Bursk, ed., *Cool Fire*
Grace Cavalieri, *Pinecrest Rest Haven* (Capital Collection)
Moshe Dor, Barbara Goldberg, and Giora Leshem, eds. *The Stones Remember*
Harrison Fisher, *Curtains for You*
Isaac Goldberg, *Solomon Ibn Gabirol: A Bibliography of his Poems in Translation* (International Editions)
* Linda Lee Harper, *Toward Desire*
* Ann Rae Jonas, *A Diamond Is Hard But Not Tough*
Vladimir Levchev, *Black Book of the Endangered Species* (International Editions)
* Elaine Magarrell, *Blameless Lives*
* Fred Marchant, *Tipping Point*
James McEuen, *Snake Country* (Capital Collection)
* Barbara Moore, *Farewell to the Body*
Miles David Moore, *The Bears of Paris* (Capital Collection)
* Jay Rogoff, *The Cutoff*
Robert Sargent, *Aspects of a Southern Story*
Robert Sargent, *A Woman From Memphis*
M.A. Schaffner, *The Good Opinion of Squirrels* (Capital Collection)
* Enid Shomer, *Stalking the Florida Panther*
Hilary Tham, *Bad Names for Women* (Capital Collection)
Hilary Tham, *Counting* (Capital Collection)
* Nancy White, *Sun, Moon, Salt*
* George Young, *Spinoza's Mouse*

* Washington Prize winners

Requests for our brochure and other information must be accompanied by a self-addressed stamped envelope.

What makes the poems in *Gandhi's Lap* stand out is the way they combine the burden of experience with an exuberant love of language. Charlotte Warren is a poet of consummate skill, verve, and moral vision. From the stunning beauty of her childhood in India, to her celebrations of complexity in adult life, Warren gives us poems rich in wisdom and delight. Everywhere tenderness and betrayal combine. And everywhere the power of imagination, language and emotional courage clarifies and heals.

—*Betsy Sholl,*
author of Don't Explain

In these poems Charlotte Warren remembers her childhood in India. Against the brilliant, seductive, tropical landscape she came to consciousness in, she sets the brittle colonial society, lost in its maze of irony and contradiction. The blindness of missionary life counter-pointed in the suffering of the native Indians is reflected tragically in her own family history—as if to partake of such a society is to absorb its decay into one's very body. Intricate, vivid, honest—these poems make no apology and give no quarter. With clear vision, Warren presents her past in all its ambiguity—love, beauty, sordidness, pain.

—*Alice Derry,*
author of Stages of Twilight